In a Time

Between

Wars

In a Time Between Wars

POEMS BY

Milton Kaplan

W · W · NORTON & COMPANY · INC ·
NEW YORK

Poems in this collection have appeared in *American Scholar,
The New Yorker, Saturday Review, Harper's Bazaar, The Nation,
New Republic, Commentary, Common Ground, Poetry: A Maga-
zine of Verse, Accent, Partisan Review, Prairie Schooner, Lyric,
Voices, College English, The New York Times, The Christian
Science Monitor, Chicago Tribune Sunday Magazine, Providence
Sunday Journal,* and other publications.

FIRST EDITION

Library of Congress Cataloging in Publication Data
Kaplan, Milton Allen, 1910–
    In a time between wars.
    I. Title.
PS3521.A48315   811'.5'4   72–7324
ISBN 0-393-04171-9
ISBN 0-393-04219-7 (pbk.)

1 2 3 4 5 6 7 8 9 0

To Joan and Jonathan

CONTENTS

In a Time

Between

Wars

THE CIRCUS

The circus was never meant for children:
They believe too firmly to tremble as
The acrobat, suspending chaos, grasps
The outstretched fingers of redemption.
Success for them being foreordained,
They look away, unsatisfied,
Lured by the clamorous blandishments
Of paper monkeys dangling on sticks.

Only their parents lean forward transfixed:
Believing in gods but knowing gods can fail,
They focus passion on the serpent tricks,
Intent upon their spangled deities
Resisting the temptation of the fall;
And in their seats they swing ambivalent
In close communion with the timed trapeze,
Dreading and yet half-hoping for mischance,
Waiting for the instant when the hand will slip,
The wish just missing the receptive grip,
The dazzling body plunging down to burn
Upon the pyre of horror-kindled eyes
In ancient ritual of sacrifice,
While high above, the restless children dance
Across the tightrope of their unconcern.

THE GODS ARE NOT
DEAD

Sorrow sweeps upward into the arch
That cloisters our loneliness, and pity peals
Loudly from the steeple of the brain,
Summoning us to prayer. Quietly
We sit in crowded rooms and pray
To private gods for personal release:
Mercy, we whisper, and as we shape
The gods to grant us mercy, we sacrifice
Our guilt; mercy: and the gods must sin
To bear our sin. Here in the empty church
Of our despair, thankful we sit,
Bowed to the inexorable will
Of hand-made gods, and win absolution
For crimes we cannot commit.

Love of our love, hate of our hate,
The ancient gods are not dead:
Hector still runs the foredoomed battlements;
Odysseus wanders the seas, foretold,
And the raven croaks his ancient curse until
We kneel before the hare-lipped oracle,
Begging a blobbering echo for a riddle
We can answer, and straining the empty sky
For a sign—look! look!
A white bird flying!

MOVING-PICTURE SHOW

You draw the blanket up and stretch out tall;
The day is over but it flickers by
Reversed, disjointed on the preview film
That promises design. You curl up small
To hush the intermittent hum of your
Projector-mind. Your eyes are closing now.
The theater is dark with sleep, and locked within,
The audience waits, intent upon the screen
Of longing. Somewhere a machine begins
To grind: the mind lights up and focuses:
The moving-picture show is on.

                             It starts
Sporadically—the usual accidents,
Speeches, the ceremonies stiff with smiles;
The newsreel, immunizing distance, ends
And now at last the picture is announced,
Co-starring Love and You, and featuring Fear;
Scenario, production, and direction,
And technical montage effects by You.

There is no tedium. The film is art.
Each scene, cut short, dissolves into the next.
The actors lust and weep and look perplexed
As they reflect you in the screen's huge mirror;
The hero staggers through the jungle-terror,
Seeking Love frantically from scene to scene,
And at the climax, Murder slits the screen,
And gleaming knife upraised, he steps into
The screaming audience to take . . . .

The picture ends and interrupts the warning.
You stumble through the exit eyes and break
Into the bright delirium of morning.

THE NAKED

As you grew older, remember how you wound
The woolen peace around your chilling mind
To pad the senses soft in flesh? And as
The daily headlines froze, remember how
The movies flickered gaily in the grate,
And you pressed your nose against the clouded glass
To shiver with the cold you could not feel?
You stuffed the spreading crevices of a child-
Implicit faith with faded rags and warmed
Your folded hands on glowing words until
The sun was posted bright on every billboard
In the land, and the radio blazed in every hearth.

This is a naked time: the winter wind
Underlines the trembling flesh with bone.
You rub the dry words of your faith to stir
The Onan-spark of a remembered warmth
And wrap a threadbare silence tight around
Your thin identity, and try to sleep.
Shivering, you like awake, stroking the fur
Of memory with automatic mind
To conjure up the flossy feel of peace
That tricks you into dreams of winter lined
With wool, or summer secretly alive
With promises of whispered silk as Truth
Trips down Fifth Avenue, provocative
In stockings and a nippled lace brassiere—
Until the wind plucks at your winding sheet
And strips you to the prickled skin of fear.

INCIDENT

Listened: in the dusk he listened, head upturning;
hound uprearing in his skull, he listened:
heard nothing and still he listened; heard the stillness
before the rain: sensed that: then heard the patter,
the dry trickle of feet as they came running:
heard his name: called back, hound pacing through
his brain: running; found himself running,
flecking his lips with quick darts of his tongue:
yelling: heard himself yelling, holding his throat
and yelling: running faster: hound running faster,
suddenly baying, and still running: calling:
What's up? he shouted: heard himself shout
and held his throat: *What's up?* heard curses, low
and guttural: eyes straining in the darkness:
felt the shape of men around him: felt
them brush against him; felt them lumber past him;
heard someone sobbing in his ear in time
with running feet: the hound still baying madly,
whirling madly around his skull, whirling:
running: found himself running, wheezing: pressed
his lips between his teeth: saw lights and flowed
into the baying mob, the hound now hurtling
against the door with whimpering cries: heard curses,
yet pressed his lips between his teeth, feeling
the hound hurtling against his skull, splintering
the door: pressed forward: strained forward, holding his
        throat,
and then the door burst open: out streaked
the hound, jaws slavering: *Kill them!* he shrieked;
Kill them!

SUN, STAND THOU STILL

And if it rains today, tomorrow will be fair;
Tomorrow will be spring, tomorrow peace:
How regular the circle of the year;
How circular the pattern of release.

A time to love and a time to hate,
A time for war and a time for peace.

Unwind the coiled, electric mind and rim
The wooden spokes of arms and legs to spin
The slow incessant circle of the year
From birth to death . . . slow . . . slow . . . slow . . .
Until hypnotized we shroud the spring in snow
And die at the end of every day.

A time to keep and a time to cast away.

No, love planted patiently in frozen hope
Will not sprout in spring; peace will not grow
In the furrowed rubble the heart will plow
When the wind turns nuzzling warm. *To every thing*
There is a season, but the almanac
Betrays the farmer sowing seeds of prayer:
No piercing leaf will ever green the black
Loam of our destiny though the clock strike spring.
The year is death; the circle is despair
Until we lock the ticking wheel and pry
The year-spun mind from alternation's track
To fix it blazing in the skull's dark sky.

ATOM BOMB

Deep in our fear, we think we will escape
Event, for we have wound our days around
Us till we are inviolate: cocooned
By time and bandaged fleshly out of shape,
We are too well disguised to die, though one
By one our brothers topple, meager prey
Gnawed quickly naked to residual bone.

We grieve the brother, but we shrink intact
And separate, refusing to betray
Our hiding place, and keeping lonely watch
With beady eye and swivel neck to catch
The deviation in our tight design
That flickers innate danger so we can back
Into the fibrous ball we were before.
We are afraid: we know: the very core
Of our own immortality is fear.
Admission saves us from the cultured whine
Of conscience, and we wipe an honest tear.

We know that death will come to us, we say
With philosophic resignation. *Alas,
Poor Yorick! I knew him, Horatio* (and they
Will know us too), but in our concave glass
We split in two and see our twin stretched dead
With candles at his feet and at his head
Guttering, while we look on and childishly
Applaud the cosmic pathos of the scene.

Never before have so many dead men reached
To tear the summer from our muffled brain
And claw us conscious to a season bleached
With danger; still we huddle in our green-
Lapped darkness, wintering a hermit peace
In vigilance. Event will never trace
The puzzling scent of our identity

To stalk our powers till we stagger blind
And childless, tripping over raveled days
To fall to carrion.

                        No, even when
The focus narrows to the final point
That penetrates the insulated mind
And strips our consciousness of all pretense
To leave us cowering naked, face to face
With imminence, desperately we crawl
Backwards on hands and knees with shrill lament:
Not now! till arched against the ticking wall,
Pointing the others out, separately
We shriek in unison: *Not me! Not me!*
Not me!

THE ENEMY

They are still there—on the other side.
We know. Crouched in the tower,
we catch them in our concave mirror,
their shadows multiplied
in the arithmetic of our fear.
They are waiting over there,
but a moat of languor curves
around the battlement of nerves
and we can sleep today.
Outside, the silence throbs like a drum
to warn us they will come
tomorow when the moat runs dry,
but where can we fly?
All we can do is cower
behind the ramparts of delay.

THE SLEEPER

He stirs a little, smiles, and stretches out
luxuriously—he can sleep when rain
claws at the heaving flanks of window pane
and fanged ice clings to the trembling house, for sleep
comes doubly sweet when wind tears at the walls
with shriek of rage and races round and round
to rake the huddled house with talon-sound,
and danger snarls until the man is warm
with peace as he lies snugly there with storm
outside and him inside and safe from harm.

And all the red brick words are mortared tight;
the wooden words fit firmly, joint in joint,
and glass may rattle but it holds the night
at bay outside, and peace flares bright to print
its shadow on the wall.

                              And there he sleeps
in blanket words wrapped thick to keep him warm.
But bolted door is only wood and wood
can rot; the bricks can crumble; glass can break,
So he must lie on straw to prick his sleep
astir before the white teeth of the storm
are in his throat. Who sleeps on feather words,
beware. He sleeps too well; he may not wake.

THE CUP AND LIP

Somewhere—perhaps just as he sits down and
smooths the checkered napkin on his lap,
opening his paper to glance at headlines; perhaps
as he picks up his cup—a little after—
somewhere between suspended cup and lip,
just as he pleats his mouth to drink, snip
the string that ties the cup and lip, that ties
paper and eggs and butter to his eyes—

The string sings out and snaps; he sinks down slack,
his eyeballs bulging into white soap bubbles
half-blown out of a toy clay pipe, and glazing
enamel-bright until he blears and doubles
the cup. It dangles from his finger, slips
and falls from circle, spinning through ellipse;
the morning paper spreads to polygon;
the words begin to stir—the A's and B's,
uncoiling, molt familiar shapes and feed
upon the page; the pulsing eggs dilate;
the butter flashes neon-yellow, on
and off; on and off; the table whirls
and flickers white; the tilted room drips red
and blue and purple as the colors bleed,
and down he sinks and drowns as circles swirl
in whirlpool eddies close around his head.

REFUGE

Words disintegrate;
The door swings fluid to moat escape;
The mind
Once bellied out with meaning hisses thin
And flaps unevenly on naked rim
Of memory till even rim-design
Disintegrates: there was hope once,
And wife and son.

No tears:
You have wept the turning of a leaf—
No tears now for this other grief
Wrapped up so mummy-round
In layers of protective fear
That a scream is but the bandaged sound
Of a clock forgotten on a shelf.

There is one refuge: there is still yourself;
Bone-shaped, skin-bound, and separate,
There is still yourself.
Creep into your house and bolt the door;
Turn out the light; draw down the shade;
Screw frightened eyes into the floor
And wait in tooth-locked silence. Wait.

OF HUMAN EVENTS

Still strange, still new,
The pointed corners are slowly numbed
By the stroking of the patient thumb;
The straight lines, yielding to
The ministration of the fingers,
Bend smooth and casually
Fit into the sweating hand;
The silver sheen wears thin;
The iron rusts into
Familiarity.

ALWAYS THE END

It was going a minute ago and now it's not;
The ticking just stopped and it's all very queer;
It should be going—I can't understand it;
I listen a while and hold it to my ear;
I shake it a little; I listen again—
It always went before; the hands went around,
The big one and the little one, and now,
Something's the matter and there isn't a sound.
I don't understand it—there is something wrong;
I look inside; I look at everything:
There's nothing wrong inside and every part
Is where it ought to be, the wheels, the spring,
The gears; it ought to go all right and yet
It's stopped; it's got me worried; I don't know
What to do. Maybe I ought to shake it;
I shake it harder, harder—it's got to go!

HARBOR

Across the salty sea of blood
Heaved by the tidal pull of heart
No light points off the compass night
To star the torn and useless chart;

To map the weed-choked doubt and mark
The depth of fear, or calculate
The sweep of wave, the sting of wind
When lashed by hurricane of hate—

No light, but rising welcome-white
Out of the darkness lightning-spined
From sky to sea, quietly there looms
The channeled island of the mind.

COMMENCEMENT

Anointed by benediction and released,
They sway out slowly to recessional,
And buoyant in the music and their loose
Symbolic gowns, they float on waves of warm
Applause and merge into the waiting crowd.
Caught by the fitful currents of farewell,
They swirl in random drifts, their restless hands
Stretched out elastically for outstretched hands,
Clinging with all their memory to friends
Once-strangers, who loom darkly into strangers
Once-friends; twining and intertwining hands
And ears and eyes in fluid arabesque
Of parting, grasping tentacles of words
With frightened suction-wish, unwinding, winding
Their memories until the campus heaves
With undulating longing, and they spin
Around in whirlpools of uncertainty,
Breaking centrifugally from contact, whirl
And come to rest, their severed tentacles
Writhing with heartless life, and weak with wound,
They yield to each successive wave, and cross
The final line of foam-indented past
To gasp upon the empty shore of loss.

HOTEL ROOM

Irresolute, I sit down on the bed.
The springs protesting in an alien key
Remind me of the other men before me
Who sank upon the bed to ruminate
And rearrange their yielding images
Within the new dimensions of their transience.
How many men, I wonder, stood up and stared
Through the dusty window, memorizing bricks,
And turned and left, and then returned, each time
Reshaping the room to comfortable fit,
And with their going, leaving behind no mark
Of their identity? How many others
Will stretch to haunted sleep, unaware, unaware?

The room darkens, but I do not move. Outside,
A huge electric sign winks symbol: On . . .
Then off . . . Then on . . . and instantly the room
Flashes in response and echoes symbol,
A rented mirror of its occupants,
Reflecting love and pain but glazing blind
With every exit. What's left of any man
Who ever sleeps here warm with certainty?
The room no longer mine, I trace a line
Across the ceiling and lose it in the wall.
Intent on leaving some private sign of my
Identity, somewhere high above the reach
Of Time, to certify that I was here,
I lived here once, I must not be erased,
I sit here all alone but brother-linked
To every man who leans against a tree
And scrupulously carves his minute mark
Into the blurring bark of history.

IN A TIME BETWEEN WARS

Now in the spring of the year
When the maples ripple green
In wind-swept water images,
I walk a landscape grown
Desolate, and read the trees
Black on the winter pages.

On the baseball field the players dance
A seasonal charade:
From glance to glance to glance
They toss a hand grenade.

The dervish girls on every street
Jump counterpoint to rhyme,
While underneath their shattered feet
The rope keeps ticking time.

The cowboys charge on roller skates,
The lassos whirling high;
The customary victim waits
His daily turn to die,
And over him with birthday gun
Uplifted, stands my son.

THE KNIFE

We have tried words before—always in vain—
To strip the growing tumor from the brain,
And still we pick and probe with words to find
The fingered root of madness in the mind.
Perhaps if we used words with surgeon care,
The scalpel words that slit through matted hair
With steel incisiveness, and cut with thin,
Discriminating strokes through moldy skin,
Through muscle, fat, until the blade scrapes dull
And grates upon the tympanum of skull;
If we could grind trephining words through bone
To bare the whitened cortex, rotten-grown,
Before the neoplasmic fingers plait
The mind—perhaps we then could extirpate
The root of hatred that has always lain
Deep in the convolutions of the brain.
If words fail us and we despair for life,
(Have mercy on us) we must use the knife.

ON MY SON'S BIRTHDAY

I watch you roll in a comfortable world
Padded on all sides by solicitude,
And I smile that I should address you, curled
As you are, a pattern of unresponsiveness.
This is your birthday. On this day you should
Have songs about the birds and little fishes,
And perhaps some day I shall write them for you,
But not today.

            Today I watch you twist
And roll across the grass, and all around
Your unsuspecting form I roll the mist
Of my fears. For many years I have heard the sound
Of children crying in the dark, and watching you,
I cannot forget, and when you fall and cry,
I hear your cry re-echoed into the cry
Of all the children who can no longer lock
Their little fists in agony, and I
Must turn away and resolve myself to rock.

Islanded by peace, I am stormed by the sound
Of children crying in the sea-wide dark,
Crying without response, yet crying sharp
And shrill against my jagged memory,
Tearing at the sand, sucking on the stone,
Crying in the dark until my obdurate bones
Dissolve and beat upon the rocky sea.

WELL DONE,

LITTLE SOLDIERS!

You have whittled your words into wooden swords;
You have waged a valiant fight;
The enemy has all been slain—
Come, it is night.

Come off your little wooden steeds;
There is nothing left to win;
Besides, it's growing rather dark—
Time to come in.

HEADLINES

Listen, mister, we don't want to buy the paper;
we just want to look at the headlines, that's all.
Who's winning today—
The U.S.? Russia? The Mets? Yanks?
Come on, will you, let's have a look.
Who's winning? Who's losing?
We want it straight from the shoulder.
Just tell us what it's all about;
what does it mean?
Who's the good guy and who's the bad guy?
We want it plain and simple like that—
no ands or ifs or maybes.
Heads or tails, that's us—nothing in between.
Come on, mister, be a good guy;
we're looking for an answer: yes or no, yes or no?

THE TOP SPINS

The restless fingers of the eyes are stripping
The flowered day of fruit, the night of light,
Plucking the ripened bridge from river, plucking
The yellow windows from the leaves of night.
The cautious fingers of the ears are picking
The fibrous words from stalks of silence, thin-
Curling song, sound-soft, and cotton-clean
Tufts of laughter. The fingers of the skin
Are plucking, the fingers of the tongue and nose
Are softly gathering the fibrous-cold,
Plucking the fibrous-sweet, the fibrous-rose.

Stretching bridge and window into line,
The supple fingers are deftly intertwining
The fibers in and out, out and in,
Twisting words and music into skein,
Plaiting heat and fragrance into thread,
Braiding thread into the string, and winding
Sight and smell and touch and taste and sound
Around the tapered mind, around and around,
Winding the string around, close and tight,
Bridge and window plucked from day and night
And wound around the top inside the head,
Around until the knotted end is plain
Against the bulge where spiral string begins—

The fingers pull; the string unwinds and spins
The universe upon the pin-point brain.

A POEM

breaks crashing from the thicket, wings ablur,
describing sky in thin, remembered arc,
and vanishes into the hare's quick fur
to pry him shaking from his burrow's dark
and race him bounding on the dreadful ground;
the shadowed word in leaf-stirred terror calls
as meadow grass yields slowly without sound,
and belly-inch by belly-inch it crawls,
pursuing sinuously and pursued;
entangled in the fingered water weeds,
it swims with fish's undulating plan
and rising lightward, springs to altitude,
bursting from surface, threshing wings, and bleeds
into the crabbed calligraphy of man.

STICK IN A POEM

A poem now must learn to beg
To play the plug and bung the keg;

It must be lathed with fine control
To fit exactly in the hole:

If hole is small, the poem sticks,
So bung is whittled down, to six;

If bung is ten and need is great,
And there is room for only eight,

POETRY-CLUB MEETING

The sibilant ladies wear their vulture hats
Perched drunkenly on marceled hair and rest
The infant Keats on their collective breast
While they exchange assorted sharps and flats
Until the gavel gently strikes them still.
They open little beaded minds and pass
Iambic photographs that dimly glass
The withered primrose and the daffodil.

The infant, waking, suddenly outgrows
His foster mothers' grasp and, howling, hunts
Release from the mad Duchess's routine.
His thin, protesting fingers hoofed, his nose
Upturning into snout. Keats hoarsely grunts
Indecent commentary on the scene.

POETRY READING

Outside in the light of the neon sun
Five little girls are skipping rope
     Down the Mississippi
     Where the green grass grows
Up and down the glance they dance
     Down the Mississippi
Skirts flaring and collapsing
As the rope whips the pavement
Into breathing like a clock
     Where the boats go push
While the soapbubble vowels float upward
And break against the brick wall
Of the lecture hall inside which
     Down the Mississippi
     Where the green grass grows

O, says the poet, the toy
Balloon of his outcry wrinkling around
His breath as he starts to read
In the quiet room where people listen.

COUNTERPOINT

Dissatisfied
Picasso nudged
the inert instant
until it shifted
front-view to side
leaving his women
triple-eyed

and cummings flung
his arms out wide
to seize the side-
long present with his
parenthesis

but only Bach
could win deliverance
with mathematic scruple
he multiplied his glance
double, triple and
quadruple.

A RANDOM REFLECTION
ON PACKING A BAG

The few things quickly rise to mountain-shape;
The tangled heap, erupting motion, dangles
Impossible with mass and obtuse angles,
Defying the suitcase's rigid gape.
Geometries of volume in dispute,
The mind recoils, begins to oscillate
Between decision's poles to separate
The incidental from the absolute.

Inertial slipping slowly into act,
Chaos is bordered quadrilaterally.
The bulging cover finally pressed on it,
The bag snaps shut, and there it is, compact,
Complete, and self-contained, an entity,
Bearing a strange resemblance to a sonnet.

GIACOMETTI

I. STANDING WOMAN

Eye rides backward
in the ticking train,
pressing its nose flat
against the cloudy window
to catch the woman just
as she looms enormous
on the instant—
Now! Now!
Desperately eye tries
to memorize the set
of her head, the dangle
of her arms, the slant
of her hips, the root
of her legs, but she
flashes by
so quickly that
straining into the blur
of distance, eye
can remember her
only in miniature.

II. WALKING MAN

Head thrusts forward
and arms begin
to flow
with intention
but earth clings
to the heels of haste
with the insistence

of suction
and the headlong flow
of motion
is dammed
by interruption.

COINCIDENCE ON 53 STREET

A few blocks west
of the Museum of Modern Art
a brownstone building just
demolished leaves
its sharp imprint on the
adjoining wall: a zigzag
line, graphing the staircase
that lies shattered
in the dust below,
links a green square that must
have whispered grass,
a yellow oblong pretending sun,
and a blue rectangle
still promising distance
to the upward glance
that draws the line
of circumstance
into the tension
of design.

EAR

Impatient with the awkward Ear,
Who cannot keep the pace of plan,
Eye rides the rim of mind's frontier
To scout intent with outstretched scan.

Lagging behind, inept and shy,
Uneasy partner of the great,
Ear shambles slowly after Eye,
Immersed in some absurd debate

Of thunder versus cobble-clatter,
Or axle-screeching versus birds,
Content to linger on the matter
Until Eye gallops back with words.

Eye tugs reluctant Ear by rote
To draw him from protracted blunder,
But tangent-strange, a random note
Deflects Ear sidelong into wonder.

SPEECH

The vowels ripple between
the stones of the shadow-stippled stream,
the little cataracts playing grace
notes on the melody
in seconds and thirds,
while the consonant frogs
squat on the rocks,
thrusting out prehensile tongues
to snatch the insect words.

CIRCE: AFTERWARDS

Hearing a stone clatter down
the hill she rose from her pallet
to peer through a crack in the shutter.
An old man pushing on a staff
appeared above the crest,
an old man but there was something
about the thrust of his shoulders
that made her press her head
against the shutter. He
stumped forward, dragging
a stiffened leg until
he stood next to the empty sty
where the dry wallow was cracked
by the sun. Suddenly she was
afraid, not of him but of what
he had become, and when
he looked upward to stare
at the window as if he could
see her in the shadow of the room
she shrank back. Because
his mouth opened into a dead
man's gape that turned black
in the morning sunlight, she hissed
her spell so venomously
spittle ran down her chin.
Her fingers clenched as she
waited for him to collapse
on hideous hands and knees,
wanting all his dissolution
compressed to squeal but he
remained standing, staring
at the shuttered window. She muttered
the terrible curse again but knew
her words had turned as gray
as the hair that straggled over her eyes.

When he knocked, first gently,
then petulantly, beating
his staff against the heavy door,
an old man demanding threat
to prop up the sag of years,
she drew back and sat on
her pallet, her head bowed
on her breast. At last he turned
and dragged himself away.
She heard the rattle of pebbles
in the path and then the hill
was still and the dust was thick
in the sunlight that sifted
through a crack in the shutter.

A WALK WITH
MY LITTLE SON

Anchored to me, he ventures forth,
Cautiously circling fact,
And as I trace his errant North,
Horizons all contract.

A sparrow flies so swiftly that
The record of event
Is blurred into a furtive cat,
Intent upon intent.

A dazzling scrap of paper veers
From line of scrutiny—
Behind us suddenly appears
The universe of tree

That downward presses wonder-print
Upon our upward glance,
Each overwhelming leaf aglint
With green significance.

MY SON

My son
Stands tiptoe
In the sun,
His shadow striking
The hour chill,
And in the mirror of his
Appraising frown,
I see myself growing down.

Proud of his height,
And yet afraid,
I, too, stretch upright,
Needing the warmth
Of a son
Who needs my shade.

FATHER

I.

My father is growing old.
Even in the summer sun
he warms his trembling hands on
my dwindling flame,
rubbing them together
petulantly while
the fire flickers and sinks into
the whitening ash of my name.

My father, I would stir up
my love if I could
but I too am cold
and I must turn
to another fire where
my children burn.

I I.

Dark with sleep I snap on
the light and meet
my ghost in the misty
bathroom mirror.   I wipe
the glass clean and stare
at my face before I begin
to shave. I shake my head
in disbelief: I have grown
much older and my dead
father watches me
sardonically, his gray
hair sprouting stiff from
the side of his head
and a little wart
blinking red
under his right eye.

I raise my hand in grim
salute and turn on the hot
water. When I wipe
the mirror clean again
I catch my son
watching me over his shoulder.

III.

They used to run to me,
their faces lifted up to my
Olympian height, and I
would reach into my pocket
to dispense the coins
for ice cream, candy, and toy
cars. Godlike, I smiled,
transformed by their homage.

They are gods now,
and I watch them anxiously
as they reach into their pockets.
Wide with entreaty, my eyes
search for the glint of their love.

SUBWAY NEWSSTAND

On the distant island bound
By alternating seas
Squats the ugly cathedral of
The underground.

Proclaimed by neon glare,
It summons all to pause,
Its promises of love
Unveiled to prayer.

Between the ebb and flow
Of sound, the supplicants
Seek absolution in
The stained-glass glow

Of gum and candy bars
And cover girls who dance
Naked in the space between
The latest wars.

JET FLIGHT

Insulated from height, we climb
Unperturbed as the landscape
Unfolds so we can scan
The mountains and the streams
With the nervous scope
Of a newspaper reader.
Tiring of the tiny print,
We lean back in the seat
And smoke a cigarette
While murmur softly flows
Against us and we doze
Until we land,
Too soon and too easily
To be alien: we still
Are travelers who squat
At home and read distance
As a book that we
Skim too quickly
To catch the plot.

THE TOURISTS:

TAORMINA

Wrapped in their landscapes,
They swarm over continents,
Memory dangling from their necks
In leather cases.
Buzzing, they alight
On little clots of expectation,
Anxious and unsatisfied,
And Cyclops-eyed,
They nibble on experience
From every side
With cricket stir
And rise once more
Gorged with events
That never were.

AIRPORT

This is another country.

Carved out of the land,
it is not part of the land.
It is an island
linked to an empire
of other islands that float
near cities everywhere.

There can be no hills here,
and the grass shrinks
from the rigidity
of the crisscrossed
asphalt runways.
The buildings are always
concrete-gray and like
squat dowagers
they wear the gleam
of chromium and glass
with solemn ostentation.

The gods walk briskly here,
grave with responsibility,
and their voices magnified
echo in the marble halls
reducing tumult to hush.
The clerks speak one language—
deference, and the currency
is time.

The winged ark
wheels up to the ramp;
the passengers line up,
and heedless of Noah,
they enter one by one,
relieved of all their burdens,
even gravity,

and they do not stir
when the roar
of the jets dissolves
distance until it laps
against the shores
of the island below.

Safe with their sins
they ride out the flood
to arrive at a haven
exactly like the one
they left before.

PORTABLE RADIO

Cushion our battered senses soft with sound
Against the silence; stuff our pillows round
With sound of music and laughter: peace is a voice
And love is a word in the latest popular song.
Perhaps there will be peace and love, there will
Be hope to insulate us from the chill
Of fear if we can hear the putty voice
Calking the crevices of our consciousness
Until we are impervious and strong.

Let words flake useless, powdering the ground—
We do not care. Give us the ceaseless sound
Of words filling the thundering hollows of
Our self-sufficiency with monotone.
Cling to us for we are frightened and alone:
The voice will whisper peace, will promise love.

HOUSE PARTY

I follow the directions carefully:
turnpike to exit 10,
then right to the light,
then left for two blocks,
then left again and then right.
The house is all lit up when I arrive
and the greeting is loud.
I take a dry martini and I
flow slowly into the crowd.
I turn left and swing around
to the right until I chat
with the hostess.
It's a beautiful house, I say.
You must be very happy.
No, she says.
I smile and move on.
You must find it interesting work,
I say to the blonde in black.
Oh yes, she says.
I step over to the right
and join the men who talk
about fishing off Montauk Point
their eyes glistening
like the dark water lapping
against the wooden pier.
No, I say, but it certainly sounds exciting;
and I move on to the left with another martini
and I listen and nod.
or I shake my head at just the right
moment and then smile and veer off
until it's time to go
and they tell me, remember
now, you just reverse directions:
left, right, right, then left,
and I drive off slowly and chant,

left, then right, then right,
and then left, and there's
the arrow pointing to New York
and on the turnpike I slip
into the middle lane
to blind the temptation
of every exit and I go
straight down the middle lane
to the last exit, then left,
then right, and then right again.

SNOWFALL AT NIGHT

The snow is falling
Soft in sleep,
Falling on the mind,
Furrowed deep,
Piling in drifts
Of silence caught
Against the muffled
Fences of thought.

THE STREAMS OF AMERICA

(FROM AN AIRPLANE)

The streams of America
squirm through the land
in nervous stops and starts
twisting left and right
and then reversing
direction suddenly
like little children who
cannot be held by the hand
but must break away
in erratic darts
to dance a design
so wildly antic
that the prim roads
which plod alongside
like patient parents
must crook restrain-
ing elbows to
nudge the frantic
dancers into line.

THE ACROPOLIS

It must be acknowledged
that in some respects
the ancient Greeks
were not much better
than their neighbors.
They schemed and lied
with childish skill
and rushed off to war
when tired of their labors.
But somehow they had a vision
of gods who were men
or men who were gods
and so they built
their temple high
on a towering hill
and filling it with sky
they made it soar
weightless in the golden air,
thus honoring their gods
and themselves even more.

SUNDAY AT THE

LUXEMBOURG GARDENS: PARIS

The gardens, once royal grounds,
Stretch far along the paths
That run as straight as the lines
Of a musical staff,
And on their holiday
The people stray
Up and down the scale
Within the boundaries
Of a minor key,
And even the Sorbonne students,
Huddled in a group beneath
A flowering chestnut tree,
Subdue their laughter until
It rattles pleasantly
On the window of the afternoon.
The little children who sail
Their rented boats on the pond
Around the central fountain
Run back and forth but never raise
Their voices in the shrill
Accidentals of abandon.
Here in the gardens that once
Harbored Marie de Medici
Students, mothers, children, gendarmes—
All move in a counterpoint of purposes
That meet in dominant and tonic chords
And then move off once more
Languorously, like swimmers,
In the underwater tension of the sun,
Each simple motif separate
Yet crossed and crisscrossed
Into a design so intricate
That only Bach could have fashioned it.

SCHOOL RECESS:

KANDERSTEG

The Swiss love their mountains,
But they are jealous, too,
And they cannot rest until
They climb hunchbacked
In wind and rain and snow
Challenging the right
Of mountains to height.
Even the children know the rules,
And when the recess bell
Clangs on this rainy day,
They burst heedless out of school
And splinter into play,
Racing off outstretched in
A game of tag, or spinning around
A wooden bar, or climbing a tree,
Or kicking a muddy ball
In the devious angles of control,
Or shinnying up an iron pole
That substitutes for mountains
Until school is out,
Or merely running for the sake
Of running, their summer faces
Uplifted to the wind,
And while the schoolmaster chats
Across the picket fence, impervious,
The children, rain-entangled, shout
And screech and slip and slosh
Into the rhythmic frenzy
Of a Breughel canvas,
But the high bar where
Three little girls dangle
Upside down like bats
Belongs to Hieronymus
Bosch.

MADRID

For a few pesetas, a guide
will take you through the Royal Palace
and in the monotone of habit
will discourse on the vases,
the chandeliers, the tapestries
designed by Goya, the ceilings
painted by Tiepolo with the heavy-thighed
insistence of his dreams, and a
roomful of clocks that keep
exact time, and since he is dead,
she will let you see the private
apartment where Alfonso XIII
read a novel entitled
Ashes of Desire and slept
in a plain brass bed.
        When you go
to the bull fight, little boys' eyes
will tear at your coat to sell
you programs and toy bulls
as souvenirs. Once inside,
you must rent a cushion, for
the seat is stone. Promptly at six
the bull bursts into the ring
and is greeted with a roar
of affection. After he is baited
and stuck and torn until
his black flanks are streaked with blood
and he halts in heaving bewilderment,
the matador bows extravagantly
and moves across the field to sweep
him around in the ceremonial dance
that the crowd applauds and finally
he lifts his sword and plunges it deep
into the lacerated flesh. The bull drops
his head but spreads his feet to keep

his dignity while the blood
spurts in a dark stream
from his nose and mouth and spills
all over Hemingway's afternoon beard.

You will find, if you take a bus
to the outskirts, that Spain is a dry
land and that the sun of the city
suddenly sets without the twilight
of a suburb and everything is still
except for a few boulders on a dusty hill
that move and turn into sheep.

GEORGE WASHINGTON BRIDGE

ON A RAINY DAY

It must be raining now—you feel it flog
Your face, and yet there is no rain; you shiver—
There isn't even sky or bridge or river;
There is the fog, if you can say that fog
Exists, but there is nothing else save where
The dripping wind has washed the sky slate-bare,
And for an instant cables seem to quiver,
Almost as if a bridge were really there.

GEORGE WASHINGTON BRIDGE

AT DUSK

It was late in the twilight,
And early in the fall;
The bridge rested silently—
Birds began to call.

Three birds flying southward
Called down from the sky,
And the bridge stirred a little
Hearing their cry,

Stirred a little and swayed,
More beautiful than words,
Then rose on wings of darkness
And followed the birds.

SPRING THAW

Behind the window pane that heats
The winter sun to summer glow,
I watch the rivulets of spring
Emerge from mounds of melting snow
And trickle down the asphalt paths,
While orange in the shadow-sprawl
That graphs the tilting of the day,
A rusty fence proclaims the fall.

END OF SUMMER

Dissolving scraps of paper flake
The ruffled borders of the lake.

Once tremulous with slip and slide,
The boat lies swollen on its side.

The cottage sags as shadows blur
The edge of perpendicular.

A window stripped of flap and flutter
Glints dark behind a sagging shutter,

And all the residue of plan
Is heaped around the garbage can,

While on the threadbare lawn, unstrung,
An old shoe gapes with lolling tongue.

AFTER THE RAIN

Just as the last
erratic drops
of rain clack like
counterfeit coins
on the overlapping
leaves that grow
clamorous
with heads and tails
the white gulls
on the dark river
rise
and begin to snow.

SNOW BIRDS

Overhead
There are no birds—
Just sky;

Below,
Holding their sleds up high,
Four boys flex still;

With a cry,
Thin and shrill,
They begin to run,
And with the swift flow
Of birds, one by one
They leap
To breast the snow.

THE MOON SINGS *A*

It is night.
Shadows of the picket fences graph
the moonlight.
The telephone poles tilt backward from
the upstretched eye
and bar the musical staff
of summer-hum-
ming wires. The ra-
diant whole note of the moon drifts by,
slowly settles and clings
to a line's hair-edge. *A*,
the moon sings,
A.

VULTURE

Up sweeps the vulture mind in black
Elastic arc, and wheels in slow
Concentric circles high against
The sky, scanning the earth below

With keen, unblinking eye until
It marks at last the telltale start,
And folding up its wings, it dives
And sinks its beak into the heart.

IN THE LIBRARY

The sun slips in and curls
To shadow in a chair.
Time whirls
On polished bearings.
The saw-toothed words are ground
Too smooth for sound
And decrescendo all around
The clicking words spin free and stop,
Immobilizing every book.

Silence, gear-notched with meaning, stirs
And interlocks with time
To spin into a humming blur
Of twin-circular design.

In this instant, poise-released,
The hair-spring thoughts unwind:
Slowly through the gradual peace
The heart swings pendulum for mind.

MISTAKE

Man is not made right—he's built too small
For everything that grows inside of him.
Everything's wrong: his throat's too dry for all
The songs he wants to sing, his eyes too dim
For worlds beyond his compassed head; his hands
Are made too weak, his feet too slow, his skin
Too tight, so he must heed how he expands
And learn restraint to starve his spirit thin.

Sometimes a man will stretch all out of shape
Because he's grown so big inside, his brain
Is trapped within his skull. Snared in the mesh
Of nerves he struggles wildly to escape,
Beating his wing-insurgent mind in vain
Against the tangled sinews of the flesh.

JUNE 20, 1969

That's one small step for man,
one giant leap for mankind.

What can we offer him
who once shrank from the dark
and cowered in his cave
a stone in each horny hand?
What can we offer him
who swims the impenetrable depths
of the sea and wings beyond
the highest arc
of disappearing birds?
What can we offer him
but words
that first released the mind
and sent it flying upward
to orbit its own surmise
and lift the ponderous body
through impossible skies?

ELECTROCARDIOGRAM

The room is still.
I lie on the couch
and read a graph
the sun prints on the wall.
Two long and slender
tentacles cling
to my chest and listen
with suction ears.
No one speaks
except the heart
which whispers its message
monotonously
and in response
a needle slides
up and down
a moving chart
translating agony
into the poetry
of line.

LOST LADY

You live in the dark ages of childhood
confident that the sun revolves
around your significance, and in
the shadow of your day I stand
unheeded, though Galileo-wise,
I know the truth as we whirl
helpless in our compulsory
orbit, and I can raise my voice
and shout the formula that will send
you spinning into space, revolving
inconsequential and terror-
stricken around the sun,
but I am silent. Genuflecting
to the pope of little children, I
renounce the truth and confess my error.

CURSE

May you move mother-slow, your hand
outstretched to urge your lover's wit
along. May you feed him cautious
phrases so he can munch them
one by one. May you have to dam
the swift flow of your thought
because he cannot shoot the rapids
of your mind. May he pocket
all your shining words like coins
to be spent in a slot machine.
May the velvet of your laughter be caught
in the barbed wire of his frown.
May the bright sails of your fancy
droop useless in his dead calm.
May he leaf through all the pages
of your silence and never understand.

ROOTS

Because you were rooted like
a weed in the parched lawn
of my mind I tore you out
as a little boy snatches at
a dandelion in the park
breaking it at the stem
and leaving it behind
to wilt in the afternoon sun

and like a little boy
I did not know
the slow way of roots
that burrow in the dark
like worms and now
it is spring again
and I find
bright in the black
loam of my mind
the first green shoot
of agony.

FIRE

Panic escapes dream
and I wake up
hand tight against
my sweating throat
to find the room is still
but filled with the smoke
of fear. I start up
listening, listening
as the window rattles
and the floor crackles
louder and louder
until suddenly
the flames of your absence
blaze up and rage
through my midnight mind.

BLIND WITH GRIEF

Blind with grief
mind wanders down
the street
playing an idiot's
monotone
on the accordion
of memory
the penny words
rattling in
the old tin cup

straggling behind
blood licks its lips
and wails for water
and stomach whimpers
begging for bread

ODYSSEY

Food City on Broadway is best
for quick shopping at night
and at Zabar's you can get bread
and milk when all the other stores
are closed; the dry-cleaning store's across
the street and the newsstand is close by.
Farther south on Columbus Avenue
there's a shoe repair shop that does
good work on ladies' leather handbags.
There's the bank too but we now
have enough points to plot the course
of my odyssey and mark the corner
Scylla and Charybdis with
the customary cross. Here where
the gray Hudson can be glimpsed
from the living-room window
is Ithaca and over the winter river
blow the Aeolian winds
that sweep me far from home.

A CIRCUS

For you my words like white
horses pirouette
to the pulse of a waltz
and like the clowns
painted red and white
they do handstands
turn somersaults
and pantomime
bewilderment and fright.
With the acrobats they fly
from trapeze to trapeze
breasting gravity to seize
the outstretched hand
just in time.
Suspended over threat
my words dance on
the tightrope of rhyme
then plunge to the net
released from design.
They clang and crash
with cymbal clash
and blare like brass
and roll like drums
till you lean from
the balcony of your mind
and applaud the pandemonium.

TELEPHONE

I sit here in my chair
unthinking, the wire of sense
pulled out of its socket.
You are far away
but perhaps you know
for you sit down too
and hooking your fingered thought
you dial slowly:
M . . . I . . . L . . .
Caught by doubt you pause
for reassurance
your finger searching
the directory of nerves
for my name.
Yes there it is.
You were right.
You dial faster now:
T . . . O . . . N . . . You wait.
Suddenly the air
around me vibrates
shrill with promise.

WHY I WOKE YOU UP
LAST NIGHT

Last night you stirred
and turned away
and I watched you in
your sleep, soft and warm
and separate, and you
were so far away
in a universe where
the planets spin around
your personal sun
that I could not stand
the hiss of distance
and reaching across
the galaxies of sleep
I touched your hand.

GIFT

No shining words; no silence like a string
Before it sings—only this grubby thing
I hold here in my hand, this offering
Clutched in my hand as a little child holds tight
A stick of peppermint striped red and white,
And clings to it through tag and hide-and-seek
To save it for the words he cannot speak,
And then looks up and shyly offers it,
Sticky and dirty now, his eyes word-lit,
And says no more but, "Here, this is for you,"
And runs away; so here, my dear—I, too,
Thrust out a sticky hand—this is for you.